THE FATE
OF
VULTURES

THE FATE
OF
VULTURES

New Poetry
of Africa

An Anthology of Entries
from the
1988 BBC Arts and Africa
Poetry Award

Edited by
Kofi Anyidoho
Peter Porter
and Musaemura Zimunya

HEINEMANN

Heinemann International
a division of Heinemann Educational Books Ltd
Halley Court, Jordan Hill, Oxford OX2 8EJ

Heinemann Educational Books (Nigeria) Ltd
PMB 5205, Ibadan
Heinemann Kenya Ltd
Kijabe Street, PO Box 45314, Nairobi
Heinemann Educational Boleswa
PO Box 10103, Village Post Office, Gaborone, Botswana
Heinemann Educational Books Inc
70 Court Street, Portsmouth, New Hampshire, 03801, USA
Heinemann Educational Books (Caribbean) Ltd
175 Mountain View Avenue, Kingston 6, Jamaica

LONDON   EDINBURGH   MELBOURNE
SYDNEY   AUCKLAND   SINGAPORE
MADRID

British Library Cataloguing in Publication Data

The fate of vultures. – (African writers
series. Heinemann African poets)
1. Poetry in English. African writers to
1960. Anthologies
I. Porter, Peter, 1929–
II. Zimunya, Musaemura Bonar
III. Anyidoho, Kofi, 1947– IV. Series 821

ISBN 0–435–90550–3
ISBN 0–435–90551–1 Export

Photoset by Wilmaset, Birkenhead, Wirral
Printed in Great Britain by
Cox & Wyman Ltd, Reading

CONTENTS

Please note that the names of the 19 poets accompanied by the symbol ◆ are book prize-winners.

ACKNOWLEDGEMENTS

Arts and Africa is broadcast weekly on the BBC World Service for Africa on Saturdays at 15.00 and 17.15 and repeated on Sundays at 21.30. It is a half-hour programme which features African writers, musicians, painters and performers.

INTRODUCTION

Kofi Anyidoho, Peter Porter and
Musaemura Zimunya

Response to the 1988 BBC Arts and Africa Poetry
Competition was tremendous, almost overwhelming.
Altogether, there were some 4500 poems submitted by over
1200 poets. There were entries from all over Africa, and
from Africans resident in Europe, North America and Asia.
Nigeria alone accounted for close to a third of the entries, a
reflection of its size and population, but perhaps also of the
vigour of the poetic scene there. South Africa, Ghana,
Kenya, Malawi and Zimbabwe also had very strong
representation.

The first two prizes went to the Nigerian poets Tanure
Ojaide for *The Fate of Vultures* – a good title for this
anthology – and Afam Akeh for *Nectar*. Gichora Mwangi
of Kenya took the third prize for *If*. The three winning
poems appear at the beginning of the anthology. The 19
book prize-winners are indicated within the anthology by
the symbol ◆.

Tanure Ojaide is already a familiar voice, having won the
Africa region Commonwealth Poetry Prize (1987) for his
collection *Labyrinths of the Delta*. *The Fate of Vultures*, his
prize-winning poem, comes through with a very compelling
vision captured in striking images and symbols of
corruption which nevertheless are uplifting and redeeming
in the poet's hands. *Nectar* pursues similar aims and
employs particularly rich vocabulary to describe hopeful
expectations baffled by distressing realities of life.
Ultimately, it is a poem about the artist's persistent and
'lustrous craving for nectar', a distillation of some pleasure
and hope, even from all the surrounding conditions of
misery and pain. *If* strikes the reader with its fundamental

simplicity of language. Yet it invites us to take a closer look at the antitheses of art and society, power and corruption.

The choice of these three poems as winners was not easy to make. Several other entries were considered in that final decision, and we had many others in the group which made strong claims as we approached the end of our judging. As it turned out, we could have filled a book twice this size with poems we found exciting and readable.

One encouraging uniformity which can be observed in this collection of poetry, from so many disparate backgrounds, is its vitality and energy. Although one can point to the inspiration of oral traditions, it is equally obvious that some of the new poets are finding new forms of language within which to realise their imaginative structures. This serpentine tongue, English, spread as it is across the globe, is being constantly renewed by living inflections in diverse communities, and perhaps nowhere more originally than in Africa. The poems in this anthology show English on the anvil, the words of poetry being hammered and fashioned into sharp and affecting focus. There is much harrowing emotion and even more high spirits and laughter in these pages. Above all, there is a human voice, speaking through dozens of different mouths – it is the voice of anger, truthfulness, endurance and love.

The Fate of Vultures is a worthy sequel to *Summer Fires*, the BBC Arts and Africa prize-winning anthology published by Heinemann in 1983.

THE

POEMS

Tanure Ojaide   *Nigeria*

The Fate of Vultures

O Aridon, bring back my wealth
from rogue-vaults;
legendary witness to comings and goings,
memory god, my mentor,
blaze an ash-trail to the hands
    that buried mountains in their bowels,
    lifted crates of cash into their closets.

I would not follow the hurricane,
nor would I the whirlwind
in their brazen sweep-away;
they leave misery in their wake.
I would not spread my ward's wealth in the open
and stir the assembly to stampede;
I would not smear my staff with the scorn of impotence.

You can tell
when one believes freedom is a windfall
and fans himself with flamboyance.
The chief and his council, a flock of flukes
gambolling in the veins of fortune.
Range chickens, they consume and scatter;
they ran for a pocket-lift
in the corridors of power
and shared contracts in cabals —
the record produce and sales
fuelled the adolescent bonfire of fathers.

Shamgari, Shankari, shun garri
staple of the people
and toast champagne;
Alexius, architect of wind-razed mansions,
a mountain of capital.
Abuja has had its dreams!

O Aridon, bring back my wealth
from rogue-vaults;
they had all their free days,
let today be mine.
Cut back pictures of shame
for I know why
        the gasping eagle, shorn of proud feathers
        and sand-ridden, mumbles its own dirge
        gazing at the iroko
        it can no longer ascend . . .

Pity the fate of flash millionaires.
If they are not hurled into jail, they live
in the prisonhouses of their crimes and wives
and when they die, of course, only their kind
shower praises on vultures.

Afam Akeh *Nigeria*

Nectar

(in communion with a friend confused)

Acres of sprawling civilisation
where, still, we seek laurels, and reap
our harvest of scars . . .
In the slow, certain death of another day betrayed,
we commune with our souls: evening pursues you
with its philosophy of shadows and routine resignations.
Desperate for sweetness, you fold and unfold,
a windy tale in the mouth of a master, or a flag
powerless against the wind, the bile
of your discontent ferments, poisoning the moment.
This terrible truth that age reveals, you are
too full of it, the agony of revealed things
is stagnant in you, the eyeless darkness
in which sad things prosper, robed in purple.
Laughter can lose its value.
Like a burst of evening wind
that sweeps all history into vague, little dunes
of beachsand and nothing, I wield a simple truth
against life's dread events.
An avalanche of the spirit has told me tales
I did not know were there.
And I have seen life so dead, unreal, openly savage
like a rogue who has lost his shame to a prison cell.
And I have seen vibrant mornings collapse
into the cloying grimness of sun-forsaken nights.

Grief was not enough.
So dim, the moonlight nights
in places where life is poured out in wine glasses,
and love is a vigorous celebration of the loins.
And dim, the parliament of letters, which
never to itself would admit its impotence.
Each blue morning by the waters of the Atlantic,
the street spread its wisdom like a tireless whore,
and there were souls ticking like bombs
at the sharpened edge of mad moments.
I am possessed by a many splendoured truth . . .
Poetry was there all the time!
In the dead, purulent places where, sometimes,
the soul pours out its pain, poems abound,
and dreams are eager, waiting for dreamers.
Tonight in our republic of lies, poetry is born again
in me like never before: till the morning comes,
my soul will light up the dark
with its lustrous craving for nectar.

THIRD PRIZE

Gichora Mwangi   *Kenya*

If

If he could have his way the artist might
change the hues of the sky and make it blue
at night

If she could have her way the songstress might
change the tune of the sad song and make fears
obsolete

But life, we forget, is the colour of pain
and pain and fears and sorrow the colour of life

If we change the hues of the night
in it we shall see more clearly
The little cricket that always hid,
The hyena that laughed
The kondo that stalked
and, glaring in blood red,
the executed conspirators that were executors once

Ama Asantewa Ababio   *Zimbabwe*

We Mothers

we are the mothers
whose eyes water
with helpless tears
each time we watch
our sons bow brutalized
to the savagery
in the streets of
SOWETO, KINGSTON, HARLEM.
we are the mothers
living in tortured fear
of the ravaged ripping
of our daughters' flesh
by the inhumanity of your crazed desire

we are the mothers
whose sinews strained
in fields of sugar-cane
nurturing a sweetness

that only you could taste
and today
our bony fingers
shine the ornaments
that you display
in the show places
you call homes
reaped from the sowing
of our children

we are the mothers
who stretch a pound of flour
into a generation
of hungry bellies
and keep the fire of life burning
in the hearts of our children
robbed of hope
with stories of heroes
resplendent in cloaks of Afrikan greatness.
and the rumble of a song
whose spirit has ever lived
in the part of our souls
you have never touched
you can never touch

we are the black mothers
of Afrika, Jamaica, America

we are the mothers
wronged by history
we are the mothers
we will not forget
we are the mothers
whose seed
will exact justice
from your future generations

Early Morning City Blues

last night
spills over
into a
shrouded haze of a morning

morning's mist
moves
over her buildings grasping for the sky
exposed
in the nakedness
    of their steely greys
        fading oranges
            watery whites

birds move
in muted joy
for freedom of open skies
before pollution
and noise of humans
out-space them

there is
mystic melancholy
over the city
as she rises
reluctantly
opens up herself
to the
yawning corruption
of
a new day.

Alex Agyei-Agyiri *Ghana*

Passover

. . . of late we are spirits
brooding on a cauldron

we carry rumours of the past
in short sentences

at each stop
we present our offerings

hanging the lamp on our necks

Drum beats at the revolution square
aims to reach a threshold

possessing the clansmen
The decadence rows on . . .

Funso Aiyejina *Nigeria*

To Abuenameh at Four

NO, son, I was not going to the hospital to my brother.
He died.   Yes. He did.
Not as in the games about doctors and patients which you
    now play
With your brother

Since your encounters with the surgeon's art earlier in the
    year.
He died:
In spite of the doctors: in spite of the nurses: in spite of hope.
He died on the last day of April::April::the cruellest month!

But we are now safely into May::May::the month of your
    birth!
And after our sad sad loss at the end of April's showers
Let us welcome back your day of mirth
Into the month on whose wet wings of flowers
You danced triumphant into our expectant world.

Child of the ministering rains of the month of May
And of green branches garnished with bird-songs of love,
Long may you survive the cruel April of the poet's calendar.

Afam Akeh   *Nigeria*
_____

Elegy For Oduduwa

That day, while he dreamed immortally of tomorrow
in the land he loved, he fell forever upon his brush.
In the cities where they rest their dead with loudspeakers,
they mourned him with motorcades and lorry-loads of beef,
their babies were forbidden to bear any other name.

He bestrode the land like an April rain,
spreading thunders and sowing by lightning,
he, of whom the baskets whisper at the marketplace:
'He raised a million grainaries in a time of want'.

Oduduwa the bounteous arm, son of Iroko,
champion wrestler of the clan, the one
with whom the rains signed a fattening contract,
captain of the forge, his furnace
fashioned an age of hungry hoes.

He bestrode the land like an April rain,
spreading thunders and sowing by lightning;
wherever he passed darkness was forbidden to be there,
whenever he spoke power was delivered to the poor.

The wind blew mightily from West to East,
they saw the magical hand of Oduduwa;
the wind blew mightily from East to West,
they saw still the hand of Oduduwa.

Oduduwa the question in whom a people sought
their answer, the beginning in whom was also the end,
they wore him in their memories like an amulet,
their stores were forbidden to sell any other face.

He who lived that flags may mean more to men,
they hoisted his face and forgot his flag, death
stood by his grave and convulsed in laughter.
In the cities where they rest their dead with drums,
they buried him with his cap, his shoes
were forbidden to be worn by any other feet.

Mid-Year Blues

Every rain, every rain, the water
flushes out the bowel of Lagos,
and writes a poem of pain.
Each grim sight festers in its pool
like an ageless sore,
until the moments bow in shame,
and the streets
are vengeful floods of errors
waiting to be drained.
The feet select their steps, recoil
from mud, deny their guilts;
the eyes searching through the wetness
are pregnant with the absent sun.
The nation tells her tale:
Each great wind
reveals echoes of the Dream
until in the drenched moments
there is a thirst for sunlight, and
in the air, a lament is born
for the prosperous paths not taken.

◆ **Richard Afari Baafour** *Ghana*

There Was Thunder Without Rain

We have slipped again
Into the spell
Of the eagles

The crisis has
Swept the voices
And the beat of drums
Onto the rostrum.

Did you not fall
Into our cries of faith
Gushing all over
The outdoor forums?

The voices streamed then
Like faith on the sabbath
Swelling the hours
Thinning the spaces
Between you and me.

Our oath with the past
Snapped, taut, in our
Fitful thrust beyond
The myths that spill
Our soul's glint
Into the gutters

We wrote off the curses
With a flash of the hand
We were swept off our feet
Onto the stern slopes of time
Where the faces
Stood naked
In the sudden afterlight
Of their season's Whitewash
And the hushed spaces
Were stripped open
And the tongues that
Stood behind the glare

Of the voices came
Plummeting down
With dead leaves

We sang more loud
Than clear our judgement
Even of the dead
Our hands played
With retrospect
We had more songs to sing
Than a new-found choir

There was thunder without rain —
Time for a dread rainbow
We have taken the rainbow
Out of the sky

We have wrapped our heads
With the wrath of its gestures.

Biyi Bandele-Thomas   *Nigeria*

Waiting for Others

This cramped little room
Is not only adorned with torn posters
of Lee Jackson and Pele Marley
But also with black and white
photographs,
Out-dated almanacs
Cheap dusty pencil sketches

and deep ugly nail holes
Bedecking the senescent walls painted
with thin tired peeling white-wash
      It is also graced with rickety-beds, broken stools.
Creaking chairs, torn mats and a wobbling
bench
On a broken floor on which
Alternate strips of cemented space
Vie with ugly laps of naked earth
and vestiges of muddy footprints
crown it like the thousand footprints
in a village square
after a night of veritable feasting

      And on an army cot
with a mattress full of bugs
a bulky figure lies
Eyes shut. Cigarette burning,
Cracked foot stretched through the
hingeless window
Arms stealing surreptitiously at whining
gnats
And mind wondering when the others
will come home
so that they will go and buy some
tuwo
from the wizened old woman under the moonlit
Mango tree . . .

Philip Bateman   *South Africa*

Cinnamon

I swam towards a hidden land
Your eyes, your soul, were in my arms
I sank into the wet, sweet sand
Uncovered two delightful palms

Now when the sun kissed soft my face
And feather thoughts were in my spine
'Twas you that drew me to your space
And I that shared some dreams of mine

Then when I kissed your peach-skinned nose
And tipped my tongue against your ear
I felt from deep a sapling rose
And whispered dreams we both held dear

You had become my orchid girl
With coral shells around your waist
Who stroked your petals on a pearl
With nectar brew my keen lips laced

Now years have passed but still I miss
Your fragrant warmth and pollen hand
I still recall your cinnamon kiss
That glimmering moon in a smiling land

I hope that you, on those sultry nights
When you gaze across the azure sea
Will turn your eyes from those gentle sights
And kiss an orchid, just for me

Charles Agboola Bodunde   *Nigeria*

Prologue

Old woman of the kernel grove,
My lines, woven like the jointed stems of tall bamboo
and tight like the skin of fresh palm fruits
speak of your large looms,
tell of the dark water of the dyeing pits
and the sweet smell of your kernel oil.

I bring to you voices in a calabash,
voices that melt into the air in four phases:

One to the memory of your smoking kernels
that turned black under the tongues of fire,
another to the large looms
and the long shuttles that pierced the grooves,
one to your mud furnace
where you burnt the dye-wood into ashes,
and the last voice melts into the sky
following your dark shadow among the clouds.

Old woman of the kernel grove,
the hearth on which the tongues of fire
parched the kernels has turned cold.
The wood on which the looms clung
now gleams with a tapestry of webs.
The dyeing pits are now filled with mould,
weaving the nets of wool in the dyeing pots.

But you grow in my lines
like the green yam tendril
shooting through the mould
coiled up along the trunk of a dry tree.

My Duty

I have spread the kernels
on the flat surface of the dry rock
leaving the sun to beat the weevils among the grains.

I have turned the grains round
to let the wind blow
the woolly nets of gathering mould.

I have done my duty,
The kernels are free,
They are free from the weevils and mould.

Old woman of the kernel grove

    I hear echoes
    from the bottom of the rock.
    I hear the voices of friends
    playing and laughing.
    I saw them
    running in circles below the rock
    Throwing mushrooms into the sky.

Old woman in the chamber of silky trees

The kernel grains are now free,
I have done my path
in the long ritual of kernel oil.

Second Passage

The sun turned red in the sky
like a round burning charcoal
trapped at an angle threatening to drop
and now we balance the oil cans on our heads.

The long mat of grass along the narrow path
has lost its wetness.
The gleaming dots of water at the tips of leaves
have melted into the sky.

Earth has won its spines of grass
their green blades are pointing to the sky
like the tips of feathered spears in an evening battle
aiming at the red target in the sky.

We are on the same narrow path
that led us to the rock in our first passage.
We are following the same old path,
where the dry bushes brush our feet.

The kernel oil drip through the narrow necks of bottles
and settle on our dry hair.
The narrow path is now strewn with broken stems
and our bare feet step through a mat of toadstools.

We are on the side of the shallow river,
waiting to cross and wet our dry feet.
The mating toads are lined on the river edge,
They are the witnesses to our second passage.

The vultures are assembled on the crossroad,
The long entrails of the sacrificial cock
trail along the flat face of the oily stone
and sink at the end of clapping beaks.

The dry clay vessel of the oil lamp
waits for the kernel oil.
The dry centre of the infant's head
longs for the kernel oil.

We are at the door step,
from the peak of the kernel rock.
Old woman at the end of a trail,
We have reached the end of our passage.

◆ **Frank Mkalawile Chipasula**   *USA*

Manifesto On Ars Poetica

My poetry is exacting a confession
from me: I will not keep the truth
from my song and the heartstringed instrument;
The voice undressed by the bees,
I will not bar the voice undressed by the bees
from entering the gourd of my bow-harp.
I will not wash the blood off the image
I will let it flow from the gullet
slit by the assassin's dagger through
the run-on line until it rages in the verbs of terror;
And I will distil life into the horrible adjectives;
I will not clean the poem to impress the tyrant
I will not bend my verses into the bow of a praise song.
I will put the symbols of murder hidden in high offices
in the center of my crude lines of accusations.
I will undress our raped land and expose her wounds.
I will pierce the silence around our land with sharp metaphors

And I will point the light of my poems into the dark
nooks where our people are pounded to pulp.
I will not coat my words in lumps of sugar
I will serve them to our people with the bitter quinine:
I will not keep the truth from my heartstringed guitar;
I will thread the voice from the broken lips
through my volatile verbs that burn the lies.
I will ask only that the poem watch the world closely;
I will ask only that the image put a lamp on the dark
ceiling in the dark sky of my land and light the dirt.
Today, my poetry has exacted a confession from me.

◆ **John Murray Coates**   *Zimbabwe*

Poor Old Joe

The Headman used to let us grow
Our mealies on the streambanks, so
We did that. And then one day
A Whiteman came along our way.

The Whiteman said 'You must not hoe
Along the river banks.' And so
We did not, until one day
A Party Member came our way.

'What's this?' he cried. 'Surely you know
The Whiteman rules no more? Now go
And hoe there! Do as I say!
Remember freedom's here to stay!'

And so we did; first hoe, then sow
And mealies grew row after row.
We liked that. And then one day
A Conservationist cried 'Hey!

All this, you know, will have to go.
You cannot hoe these banks.' And so
We did not. Perhaps one day
Another boss will come our way.

James Putsch Commey *Ghana*

Our Black Stars

My wad from Dad grew so lean
It whittled and died with slim disease
And now I foam
And now I roam
Navigating bends of a long long month

But these canting Dads never go hungry
Their hands are ever in the bowls
Full filled through the sweat, the toil
Of fading shadows in dark alley ways

And so the virus of our misery
In the test tubes of their sorcery
Mutates into gun-toting zombies
Who destroy our lymphocytes,
What is left are our voices

Muffled in crusts of croaking whispers
Croaking whispers in mournful song
Mournful song that numbs our pain

The map! The map! where is the map?
That cocoyam[1] map of dark dark spots
Of cocoyam Dads in shells of steel
Their bellies ache with greasy fat
Their bellies ache, our black Stars
O these our black, black Tsars
In penance we implore you thus:
Spare us your dreadful wrath
Our eardrums shatter with daunting echoes
Of spades turned into big spoons;
Spades are big spoons we now know

But why forget, ye Messiahs of blinding lightning
That when a bird remains on a tree too long
It gets nothing but deadly stones?

[1]cocoyam: potato-like root vegetable, shaped like a map of Africa;
used colloquially to mean 'bogus'.

Jonathan Cumming   *Zimbabwe*

Greendale, Harare

('We're more British than the British')

There stand no faerie towers;

Only the noon air ticking, null
Through its flat breeze,
And the bleached-season smell

Of dust from shattered leaves;
At the bone-concrete base
Of one derelict reservoir.

Our sun, long drawn pale as a pane-pressed face,
Has diffused through the sky to snow light of such texture
That shadows flake white and lay everything bare.

A girl too young
With ambivalent hair
Cycles on slowly, dreamy

Into my past
Back down the road below.
The hair did not bob.

In a while,
with thoughts for a cool cream bungalow,
I will follow;

In a while . . .

Achmat Dangor *South Africa*

European Effigies

(An African Abroad)

Amsterdam

You are struck
by the beauty of their cities
and the beauty of their women,
eyes that laugh roughly,
diamonds in the gloom,
both promise a sweet
and ancient decay.

The cold outside
sears your summer lungs
and like any exile
you long for home,
that is customary now.

Figures skate upon frozen rivers
and leave plumes of laughter
like frozen pennants in the air.
There is no expectation
beyond a supper of broth
and a glass of wine,
their happiness
is an ordinary thing.

When night falls
the air is still,
free of the friction

of metal screeching on ice,
bridges span black canals
that hide the death
of ancient waters
now dully stirring
the clichés of history
far below.

Where are the slender trees?
I ask, already out of breath,
that cast solitary shadows
upon the ground?
I am offered instead
a slender woman,
frozen in a window,
she casts no shadows,
for it is too late.
But the sadness
is astonishing still.

Journey to Glasgow

We journeyed 'through
the coldest winter in
living memory',
pale sunlight
upon a sea of snow,
a scarecrow
solitarily crucified
in a field
where there were no crows.

Across from me
different eyes
(is he the 'Paki'?)
looked out upon
that indifferent history,
a man whose face
teemed with memories
of Asian landscapes.

Mists of heat
and lazy mynahs, perhaps,
drifting through skies
more ancient with warmth
than the frozen effigies
we saw outside.

Then he wiped
the mist from the window,
like dust from an eye,
and saw again
our hybrid skins
wrapped in the mystery
of foreign clothes.

He shut his refugee mind
and went to sleep.

Places of Stone

for Mzwaki Mbuli

We can remember him
without stirring songs
or heroic verse,
defer to the critics
'art is about images,
not reporting people
chained in stone',
abandon him
to the narcissistic horror
of being alone, alone.

But I have come to report:
our brother Mzwake
is missing,
he left his place of refuge
to have a beer
to sit in the sun
to watch people go by,
to listen
to the noises
in the street

We searched
his hiding places,
'He sleeps in Soweto
on Tuesdays,
or is it in the city?
Look in the places
of Thursday & Friday,
he had strange ways
with his days, you see?'

Did they shoot him, already?
cut him up blow him up
throw him from a moving car?
Did he die
'in an unrest incident
reported last night?'
Now he seeks refuge
in our ability
to hope-against-hope

Is he alive somewhere
in a place of stone?
we hope-against-hope.

Kofi Dondo   *Ivory Coast*

Akosua Oye

When your wick turned smoky
And the light ceased glowing
When the sea around you burned
Drowning you in the ecstasy of pain
Where was I, Komla
Who looks but does not see
And hears but does not know?

My lioness
There is for you a permanent procession
While ants grope for cracks
By the tongue of your hoe
In the hard dry ground

And the birds hop from branch to brush
Scratching for the grain offerings
Of your sweat.

We could not even share my love
Saved in the vaults of Resolutions
So I watch the skies. I wait
For the heavenly negotiators
Of your release
From the exile of Hades.

Till then
To your memory
O mi vida
I swear
when you 'deportees' reclaim a place
You will find me there.

Patrick Ebewo *Nigeria*

Self-Portrait

I know why
> I cannot grow taller than this
> That cassava basket pressed me flat

I know why
> I cannot grow fatter than this
> The fattening room is ancient myth

I know why
> My body aches
> The bamboo bed caresses the joints

I know why
> I cannot tuck in my only shirt
> My trouser bottom is ulcer-ridden

No tree ever rears its head
Where the baobab spreads her wings
No baboon picks the crumbs
Where the King baboon is not asleep

I know why
> I must not be sane today
> Being crazy is my only right

I cannot grow taller than this
My ladder is upside-down
So I would be nearer the bottom
Should I happen to fall from the top.

Godwin Ede *Nigeria*

A Writer's Pains

Stab me straight to the heart,
Cut, slash at my entrails
Lay me open, mutilate me!

Preserve me in salt welts
Irrigate me through and through
From shore to shore

Plumb my marrows deep
carve me up;
Let me smart and twitch.

Sectioned, I pulse for union:
May the blood ooze, stain you red,
Suffuse me in sacrificial flood;

These rites will not earth me
I die all over –
Spiritual ecstasies.

And even as you stare in horror,
Death lines, pained incisions in ink
on my innards spread

You should see magnified against calm'd blood
As I die
And stare with a god's eye.

Ezenwa-Ohaeto *Nigeria*

It is Easy to Forget

Memory is the weapon
that I mount like primed guns
To remind you of the borrowed hopes
Which you grabbed from my palms,

Memory is the weapon
that will explode soon
To reveal the hate you hide
within the cloak of a sweet tongue,

I live too close to pain
poems of pain torment me
I feel the pain as I talk
I feel the pain as I sit
I feel the pain as I write
poems of pain haunt me
I am too close to pain,

It is easy to forget
the travails of the hunter
when the meat sits enticingly
On a bowl at dinner time,

It is easy to forget
the labour of the labourer
when the contented owner
relaxes on the painted porch
of the architectural mansion,

It is easy to forget
the love of a soul
When knives of hate
Have cut the harmonic bond
and eyes now see those flaws
Formerly tinted by screens of emotions,

It is easy to forget
the sting of a writer
When he rots in the womb of penury,

It is easy to forget
when verbal pellets are fired South
that beside the Niger and Benue
they also bury sensitive minds alive,

The only Messiah we need now
is a bullet in the scrotum of a tyrant,

the only Messiah we need today
is a grenade in the anus of a dictator

the only Jesus Christ we need this minute
the only prophet Mohammed we need this second
Is a fist that will smash the lies,

Memory is a weapon
that lurks in the shadows
waiting for that precise moment
When the lies have been padded
To burn off the rotten flesh.

Bode-Law Faleyimu   *Nigeria*

Persecution

The day before
as the bushpath shrubs
perform ablution
with the dawn's dew
I jumped out of my mat
in resurrection with the
holiest grandson of David
for on good friday
I dreamt of being
mocked, tried, disowned
buried a foot below
in the earth's entrails
that at one time forgotten
engulfed my sinful placenta
(at the genesis of my
first annointment head-toe
in holy palm-kernel oil)
after a formalised persecution
and nailed to an iroko[1] tree
in distressful embracement . . .
but there was no Magdalene
at my hut's doorstep
nor a faked Thomas
to doubt my staged resurrection
and to observe closely
the rotten wound
on my feet's soles
so I attributed this euphoria

to my ritual abstinence
from tasting the flesh
on a biblical friday
for I never rode into
Abuja² astride a pregnant goat
like he did on a precious colt
into the promised land.

¹iroko: African teak said to be inhabited by roguish fairy to whom
offerings are made
²Abuja: Nigeria's new capital

Songs of Abiku¹

He was born
    clan's first son
    in the festival of the corn
    of the abysmal sea faction
    womb intruder at the junction

Herbalist divines
    the storm passed away
    alas! the rainmaker went astray
    don't let him die
    when the dew drops dry

On her back mother sings
    fruit of my animation
    don't live up to malefactor's expectation
    I will buy colourful garments
    adorn you with ornaments

Father on the local Xylophone
    future hunter of lion
    put its bone in his concoction
    for him to be strong
    and brave before the throng

But Abiku's song was contrary
    may I not live long
    for me to feel young
    in preparation for my next intrusion
    so mother waits for me at the junction.

[1]Abiku: spirit child said to die and be reborn in a repetitive cycle

◆ **Francis Faller**   *South Africa*
  _____

The Refugee

To affirm a simple joy, he's told, is futile;
they own the night who demolish and kill.
They lure him into the solace of oppression –
into silence, or murmurs of laconic guilt.

Commissars and graders drive his language flat:
they'll brook nothing too high, nothing too deep.
Thus his settlement and tongue are mangled,
thus the stiff creases in his speech.

Thousands homeless, without address tonight –
and he has rhyme, anger, and a tottering roof.
What cruel allegiance will he cultivate
when they hound his dialect into the bush?

All expression collapses into solitude
when it is his own house being razed,
when identities are scattered round like junk
and each voice is burnt to common ash.

Beyond the clamour he builds one hovel more
to house awhile a stubborn victim's tale.
It offers little shelter, his ramshackle verse;
a squatter's lean-to, it's easily assailed.

But he has learnt from the sovereign multitude
to resist demolition of the crudest shack.
A refugee is never lost. He builds,
with buckled stanzas, or a few rough planks.

Another Dawn

Reveille sounded by the screeching tyres
of insomniac police vans.
An urban sparrow — unsure of regulations —
chirps a summons to the sullen land.

There's a lone attempt at verve; doves
warble themselves into delirium,
but a breeze, lashing like a quirt,
compels the erotic doves to chuck it in.

Thin cloud and listless cold prevail.
All creatures have slashed their repertoires.
The moon mopes, as loathe to leave the sky
as an alcoholic his all-night bar.

So much at stake! And bursting with news,
the sun throws up handfuls of grey.
But, to prolong the gloom, exhausted stars
flutter through a last, hoary cabaret.

To no applause. You'd think some heroine
would storm the trees, unfurl the scarlet banner!
Instead, the hours resist their nakedness
with shadows, coyly placed. A dull striptease

follows, and a skinny day bungles in.
The sparrow, the police alarm are whining.
Oppression rules, and nature's not immune.
It's now a threat to let the sun go shining.

Those Treacherous Words

I will never deny myself.
I will never stop
my journey into life.
Through these dark hours
of brutal ignorance
I toss in sheets
of razor-wire
while panic stalks the road
and tears my calm to shreds.
My memories lie buried
in a filthy jail.
Those who pretended friendship
have jettisoned
their sanctimonious poise
and, driven wild by lust,

they rape the country
as if she were a drunken whore
and she writhes blindly on the floor,
not knowing who is taking her.
On these freezing summer nights,
between curses and screams,
I hear a soothing voice –
a voice flapping on the wind –
that whispers: 'Come to me,
come across the blood-red sea
and leave the slaughterhouse forever.
Rinse the guilt from your skin
and scour out your heart's black shame.
I'll drown you in anonymity;
you'll live as if nothing could change.'
A voice as easy as a gently slapping sail.
I scour my tongue
with soiled hands
so that it will become too rough
to dabble among those treacherous words
and pollute –
like a petty thief –
my country's
authentic grief.

Femi Fatoba *Nigeria*

They Said I Abused The Government

The other night (and that's not the first time)
The police came to drag me away from home
And locked me up at the mercy of the government
They paraded me like a criminal
And made mouth like túùkú[1]
To tell me and the world
That I abused the government.
How I wish I had a mouth and the right words
To insult, abuse and mock the government;
To say the government is deaf
To the cries of the people
To say the government is blind
And does not see where she is going
That the government is a cannibal
Killing and eating her own children!
Who am I to abuse the government!
I, a common slave of the government.
Let me describe to you
What makes me a slave of the government:
When I am allowed to work, my wages are delayed
After the delay, my wages are docked
After the docking, my wages are denied
After the denial, I am told to work,
I dare not go on strike
For fear of being proscribed for life.
I am sent to school
And told not to ask questions
Hard as I work the farm
I am denied food from the harvest
I am made to build mansions for others

But denied a roof over my head
I tend the loom but
I am sent to festivals in rags.
A slave is the football of his master, and
I have been used for economic goals for ECOWAS[2]
And for religious penaltics[3] of the O.I.C.[4]
For diplomatic corner-kicks with Whitehall
And for dubious throw-ins at the Whitehouse
Not to talk about spot-kicks with the Kremlin
And counter-kicks with Pretoria.
Yet I always get the red card
For foul plays committed upon me.
Well, is it not the pantry privilege
Of a slave to abuse the master?
So if you know any kinds of abuses
If you know hidden truths
Which would jolt the government
Send them to me in confidence
For I would like to commit that offence
For which I have been punished.

[1]túùkú: red river-hog
[2]ECOWAS: Economic Community of West African States
[3]penaltics: penalty and politics
[4]O.I.C.: Organisation of Islamic Conference

Harry Garuba   *Nigeria*

Fragments

(for Mimi and other fragments of Her)

> The night is dark
> The waters are deep
> And the lost child flounders
> Between the dark and the deep.

an orchestra of images
a sea hum of drums
soul symphonies

> (wingless birds, in bikinis
>   adorned with brocades)

Surf and sand
the sparkle of the sea . . .
serenity spreads its magic on the waves
cleansing them of the high tide of passion

Today solitude rides on waves of anguish
The lonesome lobster finds its kind in the deep.
The flustered fish finds the fatal friend of the bait (Delete)
But I, in the cavern of my soul, find only the brine of sorrow
Which neither the full seawind nor the melody of a song
Can assuage

> The night is dark
> The waters are deep
> And the lost child flounders
> Between the dark and the deep.

my soul is the terrain of hurricanes
the debris of their aftermath
are the images that stalk my day

Let me mutter my life along
chant discordantly with the waves
rattle with the evil winds of owls
violating the soul

> The night is dark
> The waters are deep
> And the lost child flounders
> Between the dark and the deep.

Now is the time when a smothering night
Crawls into the soul enwrapping its light
In a cone of darkness and ashen b—light
A celestial grief grips the universe
Congealing into a tumour of sorrow, malignant and perverse

Purify the song O Priestess of love
Purify the skies O Priestess of song
Purify the universe and order this tangled net of stars.

Arthur K. de Graft-Rosenior   *Sierra Leone*

The Turn-Coat

The moon flash'd in my eyes
And brighten'd my sight
Sweat seeped into my cuts

Burning in strength of pain
He watch'd from the other side
As I work'd
I could see the light in his eyes
Reflected from the tear drop in mine
He touch'd me thro' the barb'd fence
As I toil'd
'Let me touch that glitter' he said
'Let me remove that tear drop' he begg'd
I felt another cut, for the distraction
I answer'd, but I still work'd
'You help me, yet you are so cold
Even tho' they offer me gold' he said
'So why remove the glitter? Mine is not the
Glitter of gold. Your eyes reflect
the glistenin' of a tear', I answer'd
He spoke in hush'd tones
And motor'd furtive glances
Casting a shadow over my task
Then he stumbl'd to help me
I feel the pain – another cut
Barb'd wire fought back
The fence is strong
The task should be done
The silent night spoke now
While he fumbl'd his own
Mind undivided, I work
To make an opening
From the other side
He pull'd back his bleedin' hands
Afraid to wipe his own sweat
Watchin' the opening grow
Into a man-size hole
I dig with my hands
Under the hole in the barb'd fence

Sweat, Flesh, blood and earth
Blend to seal the cuts
I pull'd him thro'
As he winc'd in pain
And took him to the shelter
On my side of the fence
He promis'd me a story
We vow'd to end worry
Many souls on the other side
Work'd with me that night
Only one eye witness'd the sight
Only one voice gave me the news.

Martin Gwete   *Zimbabwe*

The Balancing Rocks

Same dripping red rivulets vomited from the same calabash
As Tigres and Euphratres from Mesopotamia –
My brother, Cain, and I, Abel
Our tongues plus, up and down the steps of the ladder
Cain, the hare, shall breast the tape?
I, the tortoise, shall bulldoze-crawl?

My brother is the overlord of a pair of the young of limb
Smeared in the moonlit wool of sheep.
He pours sky-high libations for his young of limb
Who assemble at the shrine of the golden beehive.
His paws ever brilliant in disguise
His whore-paws hop from disguise to disguise,
A cart without stallions is his invention.

He at age-grey dawn flows to solemnize with the sands of the
    races;
Is drained out at the orange river of light.
His nest is egg-laid with gold.
What with tethered limbs, wink-tight stars, pig-grunts,
He does not bid farewell to the shade
To run pebbles on his head,
Yet swallows a thousand seeds at harvest time and over,
Round the clockwise tournament.

I am the overlord of a pair of the young of limb
Smeared in the bowels of the patched cow-hide.
I pour slashed sky-high libations for my young of limb
Who assemble at the shrine of the leaden beehive.
My paws disguise by the hour-glass
My paws hop from disguise to dust,
My limbs never woo the wheel-chair.

I at age-grey dawn flow to solemnize with the sands of my race
And drained out at the orange river of light
My nest is the polluted segregated abode of calamities
Clobbered with the stench of enforced serfdom –
My shackle-free limbs, cave-mouth stars, yawning mouth –
I bid farewell to my shade
To run hot pebbles on my head
I swallow two hundred seeds at harvest time or none at all,
Round the clockwise tournament.

Sun up and sun down, our rabid fettered
Tongues burn the roof over our heads.

My brother is the spike-like living grass
Painting out sunlight over the edge
And looting the green ware-house clean;

I am in the sacred heart of Mother Earth,
Yet the cacophony of a jungle drum
Trembles in my snow iron-charity shelter.

My brother horse-drives me through the aggrandized furnace,
Raises eyebrows to the vultures gnawing at my heart,
Measures the path to infinity with this purposeless umbrage,
Rat-digs our heart to heart reed;
I succumb to the Sword of Damocles.

Chenjerai Hove   *Zimbabwe*

Nursery Rhyme After a War

fig tree fig tree
where are the figs?
fig tree fig tree
where are the leaves?
I will wait for the figs
I dare wait for the leaves

I will come with my sister
I will wait with my sister
for the fig and the leaf

fig tree fig tree
where is my brother?
fig tree fig tree

where is my warrior?
I will come for my brother
it is here that my warrior died

I will cry for my brother
I will wilt with my warrior
for the song and the dance

fig tree fig tree
where are the figs?
fig tree fig tree
where is my brother?
I will come at sunrise
to sing this song
for my brother
for my fig.

To the Wielders of Flags

to you
leaning on the rock of the republic
men, women wielding gravity in your palms
young men swathed in glaring apparel
maidens smelling of history's latest perfumes,
hear the call of those under the rocks
listen to deserted hearts
hearts in retreat
weary soles walking the bush path
not of retreat
from the victims of the world's shrapnel,
but advance to the moulding of sweat

or else
perfumes of rotten glory drown infants
rabid teeth of political leopards of weariness
spread mats of claws
tearing youthful veins.

Accounts of state refuse to balance,
and veins bleed hope.

To you
leaning
leaning on the rock of state
contain the whirlwind
burn the flame of poverty
burn the flag of poverty on infants' faces
and tread the thorns of your people,
you who lean on the rock of the republic

or accounts of state smell of bad conscience
while wielders of state flags
sit, sigh, village bullies
yawning in political parables
murdering in speech and desire
those fragile victims
die buried seeds.

Judy

(For my friend, Judy)

Last night, it rained.
    The wind wept
like a woman with a dead
    girl in her arms.
The storm shook this mango tree
    until an unripe fruit
fell with a thud into the mud
    below. I tried to bolt
the windows of my mind, but . . .

Hers is not a memory
    You can push aside
like a book you are tired
    of reading and go to sleep.
The paragraphs of her life
    Spread open in the mind
like the petals of a sun flower
    haunted by an ugly butterfly.

Judy, our crescent crackles and crawls with cars.
    Under the blue light of the street lamp
where you played so often with other little children,
    Men and women gather like insects
around an electric fluorescent tube.
    In front of your salon, fifty women
With dishevelled hair dirge sadly and softly

for you. I see a hundred other faces
disfigured by grief. Lord, must I go on
    and paint this portrait of pain?

But do our neighbours know the secret
    behind this poem? Do they know
why I grieve so much; why I sit up so late
    writing this tinsel epitaph?
Do they know what every child means to a poet?

    This is March. Soon it will be April.
Judy, in April, the hills are green and beautiful.
    I turn my mind towards the hills
And climb, for I have seen seasons worse than these.
    I walk on, trying hard not to recall your face,
Knowing as I plod this enamel landscape, that:
    All roads lead to the grave.

Caskets

Cousin, your casket glinting in the sunset
Is Life's eternal answer to the question mark of Death.
The muscles screaming with sweat from the armpit
Of this evening are the pillars that must hoist up
The Truth you planted, a defiant flag, on the pole
Of History. Your butchered limbs we have buried.
But your head, the house of your dreams, we have
Unearthed, to place, a trophy and relic
In Time's triumphant Pantheon. Rest.
Your legend is the journey of the Sun across the sky

An endless thing defiant to the envy of the seasons.
Rest. For we have borne your body from myth to
Myth-centre of the land. Yes, with these sticky hands,
We have swaddled it with shrouds, though
The red fluid still seeps through the white bandages
And the bones through the flesh, peeping at those
Who wash their hands again and again and again.
Cousin, now that they have washed their hands
With your blood, let it quench their guilt. Rest.

Soniya

I

Soniya, if you ever see this sonnet
Shining like sadness between the eyelids
Of some dumb anthology published
In the heart of Gt. Britain by Penguin Ltd.,
Know that the sun has set over our love.
Know that I am now a sun-stoned statue
Stranded in the arm pit of that valley
From which we laboured up the hill
At dawn hoping to return at sunset
With rings around our fingers.
Know, Soniya, that I am now stuffed with grief
Like that scarecrow in yonder cornfield
On whose shaven skull the evening birds
Drop with measured skill, their scented dung.
And that, my love, is why; propelled by
The riotous passions of a bruised ego,

I scribble this sonnet with a bitter hand
Knowing what the dusk can bring: the sympathy
Of crickets and a dialogue with mosquitoes.

II

We came here at dawn, our feet sandalled with dew.
We came here to romp, like rabbits until dusk.
But you left at noon. Soniya, between your leaving
And the blue mist of this evening, a century
Has passed. And I am still here, rooted
To this valley rugged with moss. I am still here,
Watching the ravens wing westwards in pairs
Reciting your name like some magic mantra
That can cement the crack widening in my soul.
 Soniya, the rock on which I sit emits a heat.
 The molten aria of a tongueless thing. A dumb,
 Numb earth aroused by the fingers of the sun.
 Aroused, caressed, incensed, excited into song!
 And then? Abandoned in mid-romance.

III

I had wanted to keep all this to myself
But you know how bitterness razor-blades
An unrequited lover's heart, leaving the ventricles
To bleed in song, like this wounded sonnet.
A rattled snake with a broken spine, crawling
Cautiously to its death. So, Soniya, wherever
You may be, remember that at this hour of the dusk,
In some lonely latitude of the world, a painter
With seven hands and a fever in his head, without
An easel or a brush, without chalk pastel or even
A tube of paint; With words, the only weapons
We can wield, is refixing the fragments of a picassoed love

On the canvas of the mind of mankind. Remember that,
Soniya, as the sun turns its back on a darkening world
And the moon shows its crescent face like a thief, withdraws it,
Steals the stars, hides them in the armpits of the sky
And, Love, all I clutch at now are chunks of darkness.

Frederick Bobor James   *Sierra Leone*

The First Child

My life
A paradox of blessings
Opening the womb of an innocent woman
I introduced her to the agonies of childbirth
But assured her success of womanhood
I am the biggest trunk
Of an extended African family house
I enjoy the irony of harbouring
The smaller trunks on my head
I am the biggest trunk
Of an extended African family house
I am the reference box
The treasure of the family in me
A blessing to share it
A misfortune to monopolise it
The biggest trunk
Of an extended African family house
I don't belong to myself
I don't belong to anybody in the family
I have no family
I am the miserable property of the family.

Beverley Jansen   *South Africa*

The Surfer

Shiny surfboard tucked tightly underarm
carrying his arrogance like a golden crown
displaying his philanthropic past and his
pneumatic future
The gold-haired heir of statuary hooliganism
proudly marches on towards the tide.

Nothing matters much. Only the tide.
Only the waves.
Let the guns roar, the teargas abuse other eyes.
Let black youth die in the dust, let screams and
flames emanate from somewhere else.
Dionysus lives only for today and his
justifiable joy of his tantalising toy.

◆ **Wumi Kaji**   *Nigeria*

The Shylock of the West

He came to my house,
Complaining
Of dwindling customers:
A coffin carver;
Complaining
Of poor sales.

Let him kill his mother
So one of his brothers
Can buy one at least
From his large stock.

Ken N. Kamoche   *Kenya*

Yesterday They Came Again

The tea has no taste and I can hardly swallow it
because when I bring it close to my mouth
it seems to change colour, to a pale red
just like blood, Malefane's blood
When they came for him and tore him into pieces

But where is father?
Where did they take him that day?
three years ago when they came for him?

They came again
We were on our way from school
Teacher had been telling us something we did not understand
He talked about Sharpeville and said we would
remember those children the following week.
And then they came
They scattered us and some of us fell
Mathela fell, he screamed and then lay still
Nzandi was hit on the head
he fell and limped home
I was hit, but rose and fled, terrified

And father?
Mother talks about an island
Where they take fathers who love their country
But why doesn't father come back?
You see, he loved us too
but mother says he'll come back
They will all come back, I know
because they love their country
and they love us

Yesterday they came again
we were at the market
They invaded the market and attacked us
women and children lay everywhere
Bleeding, moaning in pain, but nobody wept
Mother hid me under baskets of vegetables
I was frightened as I watched from my hiding place
I felt a deep pain in me
and I wanted to cry out loud
But mother stared hard at me
she said son, don't cry, we cannot afford to cry,
we have shed enough blood already
and if we shed tears we would dry up,
crumble into dust and they'd sweep us down the mines
And then who will receive the fathers
when they come back
when they come back from the accursed island
singing songs of joy, songs of freedom?

Yes, they came again
but we did not cry
we could not
and never will!

Lawrence Karanja   *Kenya*

Jacaranda Tree

This morning
My father showed me a big Jacaranda tree
He said to me
Son
When I was young and strong like you
I dug a big hole where that tree stands
I added some red soil and some manure
I watered the young tree during the drought
The tree grew into a big tree you see now
Carrying branches and foliage
Attracting bees and butterflies from all over
My son
He said to me
This is how our country has developed
You are young
Take care of this country
After lunch
I took a nap
I had a dream
I saw the whole country on an ox-cart
It was a marvel of a wonder to see
Too precious to tamper with
The cart was moving up a steep hill
Slowly and slowly
The bull drawing the ox-cart looked tired and weary
The load was too heavy for the bull
The bull sagged a bit
The cart moved back a bit
The people behind held the cart momentarily
When the bull relaxed

They jumped aside pulling back the ox-cart
The ox-cart rolled down the hill
Pulling the bull down the hill too
Crashing and breaking into thousands of pieces
Next, I saw a child with running nose
Crawling and filled with hopelessness
Trying to pick up the pieces.

◆ **Kolosa Kargbo** *Sierra Leone*
────────────

The Captain's Daughter

All canoes like the fatigued sun heading home,
We go cat-walking among minnows
Motionless, a baking school on fuming rocks.
In our hurried descent are handfuls of the fish
To feed the long-journeyed
Waves stretching on shoreline.
                                    We roam
Among the buxomly fish-women,
Among their baskets and harsh, jolly banter
Flung at heady whiffs of brine, rum
And melting tar.
                    Among
The fishermen chanting in tortured tune
To the rhythm of their cordy biceps, homing out
Of the curling crests the day's bounteous catch.

The sun gone, the moonlight young, we come
Again to the warm sands, to imitate the place
Of our final rest – we who were there when

they took her up the hill to sleep on the bones
Of her ancestors – but break up like a stricken
Mackerel shoal at the silent, slicing
Approach of kawureh[1] when in the half-light
At the alcove, among the coconut trees, we glimpse
The tattered captain who last year burnt
His nets, buried his tack and hooks, smashed
His engine and the craft bought with the dowry
Of his only daughter gang-raped in thuggery –
On campus in triggered response to her placard
Flashed in the ruler's face: *where's our unity*
Freedom and justice in the coat of arms?

After the trip to the morgue register where her
Tag number led mourners to her icy chamber
The old man got a letter.
Beside the half-filled bottle sender found
Hours after, still stained with foamed mineral
Water, a lone valium. 'It was poised,' he said,
'On the worn lino's serrated edge
As if too shy to go under.'

[1]kawureh: The name of a predator-type fish

How We Lose Them

Yesterday, at noon, I saw five men
On the busy highway, in tatters
Clutching rags, their heads shaven
By some old, caring asylum attendant
In disguised neurotic glee.

They moved along under the sun's indifferent
Glare, and with no coin or tear to be spent,
Smiled in unison at rich lives wasting in a
Tendril-lean time. (Or was it just a big
Unified grin at the dim memories of cost-
Cleaving retrenchment?) Five men . . .
And today, at dawn, they strap five more
To drums playing no tune for infants
Or the dead, but with the soggy
Sandbags only feast like the men
On every streaking slug.

(And their executioners?)

Five more men!

Bayo Lawal   *Nigeria*

Vituperation: Prologue

(To be chanted to the rocking rhythm of dùndún drums)

More things my mouth can do than mere munching:
I can pierce with the dagger of my teeth
I can soothe with the balm of my lips
I will lash with the whip of my tongue . . .

I can anoint justice and truth
With the melodious ornament of onomatopoeia
And make wisdom stalk
In the bright alley of allegory.

I can pierce with the dagger of my teeth
I will lash with the whip of my tongue.

I can give honesty the prowess of proverbs
To damn the caprices of cruel kings
And dazzle the drunken eyes of tyranny
With the lightning of litotes.

I can pierce with the dagger of my teeth
I will lash with the whip of my tongue.

I will run rheum of rhyme
On the flimsy cloaks of hypocrites
And flood the restless noses of rogues
With the pungency of powerful puns.

I can pierce with the dagger of my teeth
I will lash with the whip of my tongue.

I will clink clamorously metals of metaphor
In the slavish ears of sycophants
And bash the bleated belly of gluttony
With the iron-rods of ireful irony.

I can pierce with the dagger of my teeth
I will lash with the whip of my tongue.

I will mount a parade of painful paradoxes
Which populate the filthy lairs of liars
And chant the tragedy of traitors
In a symphony of smiling smiles.

I can pierce with the daggers of my teeth
I can soothe with the balm of my lips
I will lash with the whip of my tongue
For a mouth can do more things than mere munching.

The Beggar's Challenge

I cannot deny, money-man,
That a lepers face
Sometimes houses maggots
And we beggars often splash
Your magnificent face
With the slimy pus of our prayers

I can understand
These cold glimpses you steal
Through the chilled window
Of your mobile palace
As your fat manicured fingers
Shuttle through a forest of fresh mint
Searching for long-forgotten coins.

When the window whirls down
And you fling an ill-fated coin
In to the hot bowel of my bowl
Whose dry cry rhymes with the thunder
Rolling in my empty stomach,
I'm sure both silver and gold you have
But you only reject coins of copper
Like the touch of my fingerless palm.

I only fail to understand
Why my collar-bones and ribs
Stick into the desert of your heart
When in the market-place
Vultures gyrate in restless readiness
To lick my bones dry of juiceless meat.

◆ **Masango Lisongwe**   *Cameroon*

Ancestor at Eighteen

The news came like August rain,
Had my importunate suitors heard?
My mother's face contorted
Several thoughts drummed through me.
    Flow tears! Flow for ever!

Where pigs forage for yesterday's leftovers,
Where the hen reads the hawk's shadow,
Where our two dogs tug at a marrowless bone.
    I'll build my temple.

The convents will reject me
Out of prudence, folly perhaps,
I entrusted my heart to him
To hide away from rust.
    Flow tears! Flow for ever!

Where mosquitoes concoct malarial poison,
Where spiders laboriously mend their broken webs,
Where crickets chirp away their grief and mine,
    I'll build my temple.

What did he die of? I dared ask
But no one would answer me
I'm a mad girl speaking my mad thoughts aloud.
Someone is making faces at me
    Flow tears! Flow for ever!

Where the mad man repairs daily for his breakfast,
Where kids tread on broken bottles,
Where dogs and goats make love
    I'll build my temple.

At eighteen you've become an ancestor
To the foetus you've planted in my womb
And since then there's been no one to care for me.
    Flow tears till you wring my heart dry.

Don Mattera   *South Africa*

Let the Fire Fall . . .

LET   the fire fall
        upon this unjust land
        let the sea steam and boil
        stones split their shawl
        spew their spoil
        on the bloodied sand

LET   let the flames fall.
           them burn every plant
           every tree and blade of grass
           every worm and restless ant
           every animal we pass
           scorch till earth heaves and cracks
           and spits its bleeding grain
           into the rotting sacks.

SINGE   the hairs on every head
           till skulls swell and burst
           till men lie charred and dead
           and no drop soothe their thirst
           let the equalising fire fall
           on us all, on us all
           in this terrible time.

ROAST   every layer of haughty flesh
           every limb and bone
           till marrow crackles from the mesh
           till tongues groan
           and fume and curse the graves
           but even in the hidden depth
           let the sweeping flames moan.

INTO   concrete city and rolling farm
           on house and shack and tribal hut
           let hurtling meteors come
           to purge the people's pride and cut
           us all to trash
           every living, breathing thing
           reduce to powdered ash.

LET   rich roast alongside the poor
           the master, the fawning slave
           devouring heat on every door
           block and trap and shave

with blazing blades the affluent breed
who die of plenty
while others perish because of need.

THEN   again and yet again
let the final fire fall
sizzling grim damnation
till earth and sea be purified
then from the ashes phoenix a new nation
of living people freed by their pain.

Land of Blood and Flame

I know the path waits
ancient as this time of day
in the whirling winding dust
I climb the crust of a rock
beyond the barbed watering hole
far from the sinking sands,
I feel the sweat of him who hates
numbed not knowing the pain to say
knowing only that we must
raise sickles against the wicked stock
who plunder still our nation's soul
and crack with harsh uncaring hands
the fragile shell of dignity.
O my country
O Land of Blood and Flame
when shall the reckoning be
the urgent ripening manifest our claim
our women weary of flaccid talk
their corn is pregnant upon the stalk

when will the midwives arrive
to free the golden seed
prepare the sacred flour
break the bread of strife
when comes the Conquering Hour
too long the thieving crows feed.
Here upon this crust of rock
I scan wide, unharvested fields
clutching eyes of children in the light,
thousands dancing, falling from sight
yet emerging anew through sheaves of corn
enriching the soil, giving it life
that genuine life might be reborn
    O my country
    Land of Blood and Flame
    Now must the reckoning be
    The urgent ripening manifest our claim . . .

Zondiwe Mbano   *Malawi*

Sunset Over Mparayi[1]

Now shadows elongate
Reaching towards the lake
That gives birth to the sun

Cattle slowly shuffle
And dust rises high
Like an oblation for rain

Boys riding on cattle
Chant the glory of their bulls
And whistle nostalgic tunes

Girls balancing pots
Yodel wistful songs
Fanning their secret fire

Men shouldering their kill
Cross fields to the idyllic
Welcome of women and children

Hungry fires on verandas
Lick pots that flavour
The home and absorb fatigue

The sun crowns Mparayi
And drapes ribbons of gold
Over the slopes to Lukonkobe[2]

Behind Mparayi a velvet
Cloud stretches upwards
To welcome home the sun

And now darkness stalks
Children and covers shadows
Skulking around the fires

[1]Mparayi: hill in Northern Malawi shaped like a bull
[2]Lukonkobe: river in Northern Malawi

Bennett Leboni Buti Moleko   *South Africa*

Sankatana

*This poem is inspired by Sesotho folklore which includes the
story, 'Sankatana and Kgodumodumo' meaning 'Sankatana
and the Dinosaur': The dinosaur once devoured all the
people except little Sankatana and his mother, who
managed to escape. Sankatana vowed to fight the creature
and save his people. That he did and he became a hero.
Sankatana is therefore today a symbol of freedom and hope
and the dinosaur a symbol of oppression and despondency.*

Sankatana!
Sankatana!
Can you hear me calling?
I call from the bowels of Kgodumodumo,
where men, women and children are congested.
It is dark I cannot see,
but I can hear piercing voices of people
crying for freedom.
I say I cannot see,
but I can feel my hand touching a swollen
tummy of a pregnant woman,
fighting for survival.
Come, Sankatana,
carry the echo of the wailing souls
in your passion-filled heart.

When bitter tears of women fill my helpless hands,
I think of you as the only one

who can stop them.
When dark voices ring,
filling my ears with agonising pain,
I call for you Sankatana.
When resistance means end of existence,
I put my hope on you.
Even when days of desperation fade away,
I leave everything in the hands of time,
because that's where truth lies.
Again Sankatana it is said time waits
for no man.

Come out from the cave and save us
from the grave.
Come son of the mountains,
while Kgodumodumo is still fighting
to lull his whirlwind-filled bowels.
Come Sankatana,
our livestock is devoured together with us,
our precious dwellings trampled upon.
Our spears in which we put our hope
have failed us.

Listen to the call Sankatana,
you the black Moses,
for you no tree shall burn,
but the voice will call.
Come and let your people go.
Sankatana!
Sankatana!
Wena themba lezintandane,
(hope of the orphans,)
wena thebe ya sechaba
(shield of the nation.)

You and only you our last hope.
Sing for us the redemption song,
we will sing with you.

◆ **Lupenga Mphande**   *USA*

Flight from the Sun

(an ode to NyaLongwe)

Don't cry my child, don't cry my dear,
We have survived this far, therefore rejoice
When we rest in treeshades to sup on saplings and sour
Carcasses of birds – feeding on death! What has angered
The gods to send heat waves that turn morning sparkle,
Engulf the land in sun flames? I always give offerings
At ancestral altar – what more can a famished mother do?

Don't cry my child, don't cry my little one,
We are lucky ones who escaped the charring glare
That glazed our village scorching chicken, cattle, goats,
Burning crops, setting forests on fire. Now only you and I
Are left wandering the wilds. If the heat monster trips us
I go first, my child, so you can suckle a little longer
Before breasts curdle – how far can a woman run with child?

From the time you were born, now you are a toddler,
Who would have guessed the Almighty God who sent you
Would also send the sun ogre to scald your feet with its
Breath, chasing us out of the village to wrestle with warthogs

For tendrils, tubers and salty soils in anthills,
To crawl in desert sand, clawing at dry waterholes –
How far can a woman flee from the sun?

Hot sand buried your father in a half-dug well
Like an obscenity, your two sisters and brother
Wilted in shimmers – many more shrivelled
Groaning, wailing out for water as they lay charred,
Sprawled out in the sun among carcasses of stock,
Even vultures drooped from treetops with constipation –
How far can a woman run in a desert?

If we have to part now for whatever reason
Remember, my son, I'm the woman who bore you
On her back against the heat, cuddled you
From the wilds and desert woes with fondest love.
Remember, child, for I see the return of buzzards
And know this rest will be the last for me –
I sense setting of sun.

Locusts

What I like most on a January morning
Is cycling across lush fields, whistling,
Peddling gossip round villagers. Fascinated,
I trail pointed hills that stretch away into
The distance, laced with shrubs and red earth.
A flock of palm swifts dart through the air,
Scream shrilly against the blue, and swerve
Hillward, sighting a cloud of winged termites.
I let my bicycle wheel against maize stalks.

In nearby thickets grey-headed bush shrikes
Whistle, looping from tree to tree; loeries shriek,
Clamber in a tangle over blackberries,
And fill the hills with echoes of their calls;

Beyond a small stream, west, a whizz of wings
Mob the horizon as myriads of alien grasshoppers
Swarm the veld, grisly glistening green, dreadfully
Eclipsing the sun dark. Shouts, drumbeats, and
Clanging of pots resound from all over the ridges
As farmers come out to clobber the rapacious visitors
With hoes and axe handles, trying to save their crops.
Within minutes the land is stripped bare and grey:
Where before bees droned in brush and green
Now stumps and boulders lie naked and ugly,
Where robins had flustered into song
Now silence echoes hushed from the hills.
I picked my bicycle and pushed into the next village
To wails of farmers choking over pungent ordure[1].

[1]ordure: excrement

◆ **Edison Mpina**   *Malawi*
———————————

Monkey Bay

I'll return to this harbour to
live my own life, I have lived all my
life for others in the past
I'll build myself a fortress over

the vast rock on which the ships Ilala, Ufulu
and Mtendere berth.
As I sleep in my fortress, monkeys from
Nkhunguni mountain will guard me.
Mphipe[1] will fry my sweet chambo[2] whose
calcium-filled bones will wave me passage
with a new method, allowing the music
of water-refined air and air-refined water
to refine the marrow coursing my senile bones.
Living here, I'll possess all my days.
Kakowa[1] will lead me by hand to colonies
of hippos, sightseeing;
everyday I will waltz to Chilinda[3] to sip lather
from coconut covers.
I'll have baths in the waterfalls of the sun here,
below an unbroken sheet of sky, a
sky without gaps. I'm longing for my life
next time
when I'll recline on my past, blurred with
news, jail and verse. My plans are packed.

[1]Mphipe and Kakowa: water birds on the shores of Lake Malawi
[2]chambo: Lake Malawi fish
[3]Chilinda: harbour across Lake Malawi from Monkey Bay

◆ **Fekassa Mwada** *Sudan*

The Fighter

The fire dies down, darkness grows
The butterflies move away
      to search for death elsewhere.
He hugs his rifle, and broods
     faces of the dead parade before his eyes
Moist eyes do not hamper memory's vision
As the heart recalls the songs of the past
      and the mind conjures images of bright
sunny days.

The rifle kills,
    the rifle saves
He tugs at the inconsistency
    and settles on his 'no choice' reasoning.
A hyena howls in the distance
      signalling in the dark a change of mood
He hugs tight the gun
     and listens to the fire in his heart
And sees a bright dawn breaking
      moving birds and men to gaiety
To a song of joy
     whose words he knew not yet
But felt himself being stirred.

In the distance, echoes of rifle fire
The present intrudes with death on a platter
He moves with his gun into the night.

Gichora Mwangi   *Kenya*

Untitled

Dark blotches on eyelids
As chimney sweeps someplace else
Dislodge the fears in my mind

I could wear a dotted brain
like note pad dotted with tears
I could wear a striped eyelid

Looking above all I can see is the little men
peering downhill at the lights
going off to declare war on peace

Are you scared of the dark?
Shall I strike a match and expose
the dreams?

Question time tomorrow night
at the owls' pub
finds my cabinet questioned on life
and its worth, we are only owls
how would we know?

Little Bushbabies of the night like
stunned and disabled pandas lost
in the dark we are groping
around the corner of the bedsheet
looking for memory, looking
for light, looking for chimney sweeps
to wipe away our fears

Waiting (for S)

Well past midnight
On liberation night

It is true that my consideration
of linked hands walking down boulevard
of strewn roses may be anathema
to the ideologues

But the cross-eyed fools
look it seems nowhere
in their search for you-know-what
Which is the emblem on banners
held aloft by the shaky hands
'Pass the cigarette around'

Count me in when clenched fists open
to let sand trickle through
to smoulder the fire.
I shall come when the flames
licking at the yellowed flesh, quiver
before finally going out

I shall come with the heroine
Straight from the boulevard
of yesteryear now strewn with wreaths
to the gods, wreaths to the spirit of
Freedom

And we shall wear laurels
With the victors over unseen enemies
'The cigarette is burnt to ashes
the moultings of vipers are on fire
Where the past?'

If you look carefully behind the teardrops
and little bloodstains that are all you can see
you may dig up the past,
exhume the memories

But watch where you place the sodden soil
lest you dampen the flickers
that tomorrow could be flame.

Crispin Namane *Tanzania*

African Demagoguery

You lifted my eyes
to the splendour of ebony
and swelled me with pride.

You opened my mind
to the grandeur of African poetry
and decorated me with arrogance.

You poured me drink;
fiery drink from the East,
and got me drunk with toil.

You taught me to sing
all these songs
And whilst I sang
all these songs
You turned fat
    and white
       and strange.

Valeria Nkomeshya *Zambia*

My Hands

My hands – oh my hands
Once you were tiny and useless
but now I call you my companion
I have grown into a big girl
I have licked your fingers
You have fed me.

Oh My hands
You have learnt all arts
I can communicate by you
I use you to cut fire wood
My dear hands
You are a faithful companion.

When I am crying
You wipe my tears dry
When I am happy – you clap
When I see a friend – you wave

My hands – oh my hands
You scratch where I am itchy
You dig the garden to feed me

My hands – without you 'am nothing
My hands – I promise to make you known
I will introduce you to the rest of my body
For without you
they are all miserable.

With your obedient ten servants
My hands – you are my star
My hands – you are the 'head'
Of my whole being
I wish the World was like you.

Pheroze Nowrojee   *Kenya*

Zimbabwe Independence

It is morning, but
The security lights are still on,
And the watchmen who guarded through the night
Are still there too, their shrewd eyes
Straining to discover thieves
Among those walking to work.
There are tall trees around,
Winning green from the departing dark.
They look down benevolently,
But the watchmen are full of disquiet:
Unused to the daytime,
Within which others too may move,
For them, even from the brightest sun,
Every shadow lays siege to their possessions.

Silas Obadiah *Nigeria*

The Man I Killed

If we had met on the fields
Nurtured by the flowing darts of the sky
We could have marvelled at the gaits of plants
Thrusting their arms into the sky.

If we had met in the forest
Armed with polished spears
Then we could have hunted the agile deer
And returned home decked with smiles.

We could have learned the secret of numbers
And the solemn whispers of distant stars
If we had met in mystic schools.

But then:
We met on the battlefield
Where corpses were the signs of victory
And vultures yearned for their harvest
And my clean sword longed for a stain
And the sheep in me craved to be lion
And so I tore into his bowels
And felt strengthened by the scent of his blood
And now by the heritage of steel
I fearlessly tread forbidden paths.

Walter Odame *Kenya*

By The Long Road

It is by the long road
that I arrived here

Like a traveller
at the end of a long journey
I have loosened
the strings of my sandals
and my walking stick
is leaning against the wall of my house

Yet how do I
relate to my children
my history
He, my proud boy
She, my proud girl

That I met their Pa, a Policeman
in a bar, at fifteen,
And I, a child prostitute

I can see it in his eyes
and he has said it often
that I had beautiful dresses
and danced freely in the village

Yet, how do I tell him
that I was busy minding children
a help hand to a city dweller

How do I tell my girl
she, a young woman
that we
those formerly of the street
loved our children
and hoped for better lives for them
Yet only the other day
she nearly died
because of an attempted suicide
on being abandoned, pregnant
by her boyfriend

It is by the long road
that I reached here
and I don't want any more potholes
on the remaining journey of my life

So summoning my children;
my proud boy,
who wonders why we aren't rich,
and my proud girl,
who couldn't stomach frustration,
I will relate to them my tale
and leave no details loose
and send them
the message straight from my own mouth
It is by the long road that I am here

Dear Child

In your splattered face I see
the different faces of our city
some bright, clean and wealthy
others dull, dirty and poor.

You roam the concrete jungle
peopled with cars, buses and lorries
like a hen combs the dirt
looking here and there
for a kindred soul
from whom to pluck
a coin or two

Dear child
fighting over leftover chips and rotting bread
does your absent father know, care
you slept in the dustbin
covered with a blanket of refuse?

Does your poor or whoring mother
know that love, comfort
is from fellow parking boys and girls?

Child-adult
your silent misery
is of an assumed usuality
no questions are raised in parliament
(your quota is budgeted in charity homes)
no public official's conscience suffers
when the city askaris
chase you off parking bays
like a pilfering rat

Child
I haven't the right, heart, courage
to tell you to your face
weep not, dream not, ask not
at what
a cosy home a responsible authority
might have been
we all stand rebuked.

Tanure Ojaide   *Nigeria*

Song For My Land

More and more the land mocks my heart.
where are the evergreens of my palm;
why is the sun of salvation eclipsed
by coups and intolerable riots?

Wherever I pass, mockery of the land:
naked trees flaunt sterile bodies at me —
my blood is hot but not on heat;
the winds gossip loud my dalliance
to embarrass me from washing clean
the tainted face of my love.

Every step I take on the land
is fraught with torments —
my clan no longer contains me;
where I am the adopted son
I am asked for marks I don't possess
before I can be embraced.
I need the entirety of the land.

The song needs the soil
for deep roots and fresh notes;
the land needs the song
to revive its strength
and raise itself.
And what celebrated union isn't beset
by one trouble or another?

I have sat through harsh winds
and alternating hot and cold seasons
but have not lost my skin;

my nerves are better guards than ever.
I have made love to all tribes
and absorbed the strength of their warriors.

But still, more and more
the dear land mocks my loving heart.

Where Everybody is King

Come to Agbarha[1]
where everybody is king
and nobody bows to the other.
Who cares to acknowledge age, since
power doesn't come from wisdom?
And who brags about youth
when there's no concession to vitality?
You just carry your heads high.
And do you ask why
where nobody accepts insults
doesn't grow beyond its petty walls?

When you come to Agbarha
mind you, the town of only kings,
there are no blacksmiths, no hunters;
you will not find anybody
doing menial jobs that will
soil the great name of a king —
nobody ever climbs the oil-palm
nor taps the rubber tree.

Of course, rivalry
has smacked the town
with a bloody face.
No king is safe
or sees himself as really great
in the presence of others.
And they try their diabolic charms
on each other, dying like outcasts
without horn-blasts, without
the communal rituals of mourning.

In Agbarha
nobody wakes to work:
everybody washes his mouth with gin
and sits at home
on a floor-mat of a throne.
Are you surprised
at kwashiorkor princes and princesses,
prostitute queens and beggar kings?
Come to Agbarha
where everybody prides himself greater
than the rest of the world
and see the hole
where kings live their unfortunate lives.

[1]Agbarha: There is a traditional Urhobo saying that every indigene
of Agbarha is a king

◆ **Felicity Atuki Okoth**   *Uganda*

The Spirit of My Land

The land where I was born is torn.
And the red loam soil trickles through the cracks like blood.
Earth's voice angrily growls through the ragged sky
And he curses us with words of cold fire.
But when he weeps, his harsh tears fall on unheeding backs.

Perhaps a dog with rabies has bitten the core of the earth
The voice of thunder and grenades are now one,
I look into the dam at the muddy waters that I dug
and lying at the muddy bottom I see the pride that I once
    had.
In the land that cradled my first tottering steps in its arms.

From my childhood I learnt obedience
And from the white man I embraced religion
I was just a civil servant whose cloak was integrity
But now you have killed me.
With a single hot arrow through my heart.

Tell me Mother Earth did you hear the shot that
rang out in acclamation of the death of your son.
And maybe you know about the aimless paths
that widows now tread. And don't you know about
the silent houses, that now stand with eyes and mouth shut
    like my corpse.

The butterflies that used to flutter to the beat of the village
    drums
Are now charred remains from the explosion of your play
    ball.

The sandals on their feet are now the homes of my breed.
Because you my Countryman, my Clansman my son are a
    killer,
A rebel, are merely a child that has forgotten how to play.

And Father Jones said a monument would mark the place
    where I fell.
But come, see the place, where lies a son of the father.
See the charred remains of the stump of wood that was a
    fire for me.
And if you hear a sigh in the wind, it's the last song that my
    henchmen,
Sang for me. And those flowers shaking their heads
Were planted by them.

Now my restless spirit returns again and again to the home
    of my youth
It is cold, and the heavens return the anguished cry of earth.
The sun sweeps light out of its house and onto the hillside
but no children run up to catch it.
For my homeland has no more children.

The old people painfully straighten up in an effort to catch
    death
But it passes them by leaving them with heartburn.
And my spirit wandering by does not ask them why do you
    cry.
For they don't know why their tears flow,
When they dimly try to recall a happier past.

Isi Omoifo *Nigeria*

Oh Africa

I can see by lamp-light the rheum in your eyes
Drowning stone-reefs in the cataracts of your heart
Speak, eldest one
Cockerels sing the approach of dawn
Oleanders visit the light in white coifs

Ah, alpha jets streak against the light

I see on your flesh the cicatrices of the serpent
Lacking heirs to stretch wholesome pipes to your lips
Speak louder, eldest one
Eaglets soar in maiden spheres
Dolphins vault from sea-wave to air-wave

Ah, tanks rumble through the night

I hear in your stomach pit the howl of emptiness
Lacking breed to turn abysses into bloom
Speak plainly, eldest one
Zebras speed on rugs of Osiris[1]
Zephyrs chase after daffodils

Ah, they go arms a-shopping in Moscow and Washington

I hear in your straw shed the taunt of anopheles
The croaks of Kabakas[2] and the clacks of Lakwenas[3]
Speak, eldest one
Gazelles strut on goldfields
Ducklings glide on rippling lanes

Ah, they clash at the crossroads of creeds from the north
  and the east

I have seen in the harmattan rage the trembling of your toes
Draping your skeleton with the collage of a robe
Speak louder, eldest one
Colobuses swing from tree to tree
Springboks somersault on the veld

Ah, they turn their war-heads to tongue straits

I have beheld in the storm-racks the stilt dance on your
  rafters
Winning a wet breach for battalions from the sky
Speak plainly, eldest one
Rivers purl downward to the sea
Canaries greet the hours with melodies

Ah, shells sing across Berlin walls

I see framed against your door the gnarled trunk of the
  baobab
None to bend algebraic light into the gloom
Speak, sorriest one
Stars twinkle in their orbs in the galaxies
Flamingoes deck in flocks the shores of the pacific

Ah, silver stars and broidered caps hit the road to
Switzerland.

[1]Osiris: god in Egyptian mythology representing regeneration
[2]Kabakas: rulers of kingdom of Buganda, now abolished
[3]Lakwenas: followers of defeated rebel priestess in Uganda

Thembile ka Pepeteka   *South Africa*

die poyie-poyie[1]

mama die poyie-poyie
come inside mama
die poyie-poyie 'll grab you
they are the cannibals
of your bed-time stories mama
their torch eyes will spot you
their oversized boots will tramp over you
mama i want you forever
no one must rip you off from me
come inside mama
die poyie-poyie will snatch you
as they did to my brother Mhlabawethu[2]

mama die poyie-poyie
they pain our townships
to pain our joy
they pain our virgins
to pain our pride
they pain our culture
to pain our nationality
where can we have pride mama
in europe we have no pride
cos we are a minor
in america we have no pride
cos we are a minor
in africa mama
especially in the south of africa
the place where i am at this moment
where we are a plural
yet

we have no pride
our eyes are burnt when we see
we have no pride
our mouths are stitched with wires when we speak
we have no pride
our ears are cut when we hear whispers of freedom
we have no pride
die poyie-poyie mama
but mama
the day shall dawn on the chin of africa
it might be tomorrow mama
we'll root die poyie-poyie out
from our place
mama come inside
the sparks of the revolution will hit you

[1]die poyie-poyie: Afrikaans expression meaning 'the police'
[2]Mhlabawethu: Xhosa name meaning 'our land'

Sobhna Keshavelal Poona   *South Africa*

Say No Black Woman

say no black woman
when they break up your family
and send your son to fight
for a land that already belongs to him

say no black woman
when they tear down your home
and take away your bread and shelter
in an attempt to break your spirit

say no black woman
when they accuse your son of rape
and send your husband to prison
for a crime he didn't commit

say no black woman
when they steal your only daughter
and banish your only son
say no black woman
when they curse you
and call you names
say no black woman
say NO!

Letter to a College Boy

dear son

last night
our house was petrol-bombed
your father is
dead
your brother
has left home
to join the struggle
i fear
i may never see him again

i hope you are well
don't forget
to light a candle
to your father
the light in my heart
grows stronger every day
we have no candles
we have no light
we have no home
work hard my son
remember
to light that candle

Pauses and Punctuations

my traffic
of words
ends
in yet another violation
wherein
the pauses
between
my images
lie locked
within a prisoned country
where
the blank spaces
preceding
my expressions
writhe shackled
in a suffocating experience . . .
for

my ideas
are punctuated
by a law
that puts it
behind bars
and suffocates it
in a labyrinth
of emergency regulations

◆ **Kofi Sam**   *Ghana*
_____

Elegy To a Land Lost

I dream of the clanging of hoes
And the distant cry of the hawk,
Of farms lush,
And fields green,
Turning brown and dry
In the twinkle of an eye.

I dream of moon-lit nights,
Of the warmth of friends and fires,
Of tales told of old women
And witches,
But suddenly waking to
A biting cold and crushing loneliness.

I dream of fishy scents
And of delicious smells,
Of sitting together with

Huge bowls of steaming soups,
But suddenly fighting
Over a fragment of bread.

I dream of happy laughter,
Of jumping and running faster,
Of hiding behind the hut
And the fun we had.
But suddenly surrounded by
Strange faces and cold stares.

I dream of a bright morning
And of fathers sharing,
Clothes: red, yellow and green,
Of gleaming eyes and envious glances.
But suddenly walking away
In tatters and filth.

I dream of a long journey
Of mothers weeping and children asking,
Of burning heat and numbing cold,
Of howling creatures and unending nights,
Suddenly ending in a land
Of tall buildings and
I, with my hand outstretched.

Gloria Sandak-Lewin   *South Africa*

The Sun Rising, Bishopscourt[1]

After that blood-red glow in the east,
A tumbling sky, streaming, scudding clouds,
Sharp points of light, winking against a
                              velvet backdrop,
Jewelled Cape Town, strung out in a
                    rounded curvature of the bay

I am here at last, poised on this
              tremulous knife-edge
Between earth and sky, man and nature,
                              work and home.
Smothered in splendid silence, I see Africa
Rise like a roar against the dawn.

[1]Bishopscourt: One of the most prestigious suburbs in Cape Town,
South Africa, and home of the affluent and of embassies

Erasmus Elikplim Forster Senaye *Ghana*

Where did Aids come from?

You talk say I have aids;
Na who cause am brother?
I need aids;
Monkey too get aids?
It jumps up and down tree top.
You talk say I have aids.
Monkey fit give me aids?
Me I be man;
Monkey be animal;
Surgeon examine proper;
And judge better.
Why, why, why?
Too many aids for the North,
Na who cause am brother?
Na who cause am brother?
I need aids.

A teenage boy plus girl meet on street top;
They kiss for one hour;
In the night,
Man and man dey sleep together,
Ah! Ah! Ah!
Tell me where?
Travel and see:
Kissing
In the toilets,
In your hotel rooms,
Sexy woman meet sexy man

Film stars kiss my wife on the video screen,
Priest dey sleep plus his own disciple.
On one bed?
Man and Woman dey play seesaw-up-and-down.
In the transfusion,
Our blood,
To give aids,
To aid victims.
Why do I have aids?

Little children write with pencil,
Adults use pen is to write with;
In the matrimony bliss,
The pen is full of ink
To sweeten the virgin hole surrounded with black strings.

Chastity reigns in the North of our country?
Are you a surgeon?
Or what are you?
A critic?
Judge better;
Examine proper,
Na who cause am?
My brother.

Sam Ukala *Nigeria*

when i grow up

when i grow up
i shall grow three breasts
the middle breast
shall be long as three pawpaws

>when i till the soil
>and baby cries
>the long breast to my back i'll fling
>for baby to suck, suck and suck

when i grow up
i shall wash my clothes
with spring water
and hang them on the roof

>not on the grass
>where chicken stamp
>their muddy toes on them
>and dogs drop spirals of soft dung

when i grow up
i shall trap the rainbow
and plant it at the country square
to spring rain on all thirsty throats
and burning skins

>i shall plant it there
>>as an army
>against the encroaching desert
>>as a beautifier
>of the ugliness around

when i grow up
i shall create god in our image
and make black the superior hue
and make black the superior hue
    i shall make the moon our mirror
    the planets our yacht
    our soles shall be free
    from the glass splinters of borrowed cultures
    our ankles free
    from the fetters of borrowed technology

when i grow up . . .

i will not be like so many mothers
who toil for food
while their babies famish
swaddled to sweating backs

my country will not be so sinful
that she will have no spring
and see no rainbow
she will not sink 'billions' in water projects
while her people sip their bloody sweat

my country will not be so filthy
in body and soul
that 'environmental sanitation'
will sanitate none
and the world would still
mistake us for a waste dump

my nation will not be so self-hating
that it will guzzle her own eggs
and break her own wings
when the gun goes for nations to fly

when i grow up
oh yes
when i grow up
i shall do many many things.

Michael Andrew Wakabi   *Uganda*

The Stone

I am a sentinel, a guardian of times
Days and men come and pass
But I the sentinel, I persist
Like vagaries of weather they batter to crush me
But summer spring or winter, I stay the stone
Men hurl themselves at me bouncing flying off like balls
But I the sentinel, I stay
They teach me lessons I learn
I teach them lessons they never learn
Me, I'm a witness of times
Times have brought men and gone with them
But I the sentinel, I stay
I stay because I go deep in this crust
I need neither wings to fly nor bees to stay
No, I just occur here and here I'll stay for all seasons to come
For men and their like are mere riders on time
With time they come
With time they go

Timothy Wangusa   *Uganda*

A Pattern of Dust

Cloudless mid-morning sun
Aslant a colourless
Slab of cracked glass
That leaned against a pink wall
And rested on a straw mat
Of brown and purple strands:

Upon this idle glass-pane
Had timelessly settled
A film of random dust

Onto which the sun now falling –

What jolting spectre
Upon the mat and wall
What dappled clouds
In pulsing rings
Along a sensory magnetic axis –

And what sudden uplift
In a moment of wordless wonder!

Willie T. Zingani *Malawi*

Law of the Jungle

'Man has decided
He'll defend wild animals
And care very little
About fellow human-beings.'
    Crazy . . . Crazy!

'For killing the innocent monkey
In that protected game reserve
You get three year imprisonment
With hard labour.'
    Imagine . . . Imagine!

'But the innocent monkey
Ate crops in my small garden
It destroyed the little I had
To feed my wife and twelve children.'
    Right . . . Right!

'Why didn't you report
The monkey to the authorities?
Who gave you permission to kill
That innocent monkey?'
    What . . . What?

'And who gave that monkey
Permission to eat my maize?
Did you, my judge, did you?'
    True . . . True!

'For arguing with the judge
In this court of law
You get additional sentence
Two plus three equals five
You'll rot in prison for five years.'
    Aaaah . . . Aaaah!

NOTES ON CONTRIBUTORS

at the time of the competition

Ama Asantewa Ababio: A teacher in Zimbabwe. Her poems have appeared in the Zimbabwe Press.

Alex Agyei-Agyiri: A postgraduate law student, Ghana.

Funso Aiyejina: Nigerian. Has published poems in *The Penguin Book of Modern African Poetry*, (Heinemann, 1983) and *Rhythms of Creation*.

Afam Akeh: Nigerian. Has published poems in Nigerian University literary journals, and newspapers.

Richard Afari Baafour: Head of the Civil Service, Accra, Ghana.

Biyi Bandele-Thomas: A student and writer in Nigeria.

Philip Bateman: A writer in South Africa.

Charles Agboola Bodunde: A teacher in Nigeria.

Frank Mkalawile Chipasula: An exiled Malawian poet who now lives in the USA.

John Murray Coates: A schoolmaster in Zimbabwe who has published in Zimbabwe and South Africa.

James Putsch Commey: A Ghanaian who won second prize for the best collection of poems at the First Ghana Association of Writers Award 1986. Has published an anthology of poems called *The Missing Link*.

Jonathan Cumming: A student in Zimbabwe.

Achmat Dangor: A South African whose publications include: *Waiting for Leila* (1983 Mfolo Prize), *Bulldozer*, *Voices Within* and *Majiet*.

Kofi Dondo: A writer in the Ivory Coast.

Patrick Ebewo: A lecturer in Nigeria. His poems have appeared in the Nigerian and international press.

Godwin Ede: A writer in Lagos, Nigeria.

Ezenwa-Ohaeto: A lecturer in Nigeria whose publications include:

Song of a Traveller, Kay Bee Cee Publ. 1986 and *The Hand of Wind*, Delta Publications, 1988.

Bode-Law Faleyimu: A Resident doctor in the Obstetrics and Gynaecology Department in Nigeria.

Francis Faller: A lecturer in South Africa.

Femi Fatoba: A lecturer in Nigeria whose published works include the poetry collection, *Petals of Thought*.

Harry Garuba: A lecturer in Nigeria whose first collection of poems, *Shadow and Dream*, was published in 1981.

Arthur K. de Graft-Rosenior: A writer and journalist in Sierra Leone.

Martin Gwete: A student of Classical Studies at the University of Ibadan, Nigeria.

Chenjerai Hove: A poet and novelist in Zimbabwe whose publications include: *Up in Arms* (1982), *Swimming in Floods of Tears* (1983), *Red Hills of Home* (1985), *Masimba Avanhu* (1986) and *Bones* (1988). His poems have been published in several anthologies in English and Shona.

Esiaba Irobi: A lecturer at the University of Nigeria. His poems have appeared in the following publications: *Okike, Omabe, The Guardian, Jungle Muse* and *Poets in their Youth*.

Frederick Bobor James: A Regional Organiser, Institute of Adult Education and Extra-Mural Studies, Fourah Bay College, University of Sierra Leone.

Beverley Jansen: A teacher and community worker living in Cape Town.

Wumi Kaji: A writer in Lagos, Nigeria.

Ken N. Kamoche: A postgraduate student in Management Studies at Oxford University.

Lawrence Karanja: Deputy Headmaster and history teacher, Kathiani High, Machakos, Kenya.

Kolosa Kargbo: A writer in Sierra Leone.

Bayo Lawal: A lecturer in English at the St Andrew's College of Education, Oyo, Nigeria.

Masango Lisongwe: A writer in the Cameroon.

Don Mattera: A writer in South Africa.

Zondiwe Mbano: The Head of the Department of Languages, Mzuzu Teachers College, Malawi.

Bennet Leboni Buti Moleko: A South African playwright.

Lupenga Mphande: A Malawian lecturer, who teaches African and Afro-American Literature at the University of Texas, and former editor of *Odi*, a journal of literature from Malawi.

Edison Mpina: The first prize winner of the BBC Arts and Africa Poetry Award of 1981, Malawi.

Fekassa Mwada: An Ethiopian exile who lives in Sudan.

Gichora Mwangi: A literature student at the University of Nairobi, Kenya.

Crispin Namane: A South African exile who lives in Tanzania.

Valerie Nkomeshya: A teacher in Lusaka, Zambia.

Pheroze Nowrojee: A lawyer in Nairobi, Kenya.

Silas Obadiah: A lecturer in Nigeria.

Walter Odame: An accountant living in Nairobi, Kenya.

Tanure Ojaide: A senior lecturer at the University of Maiduguri, in Nigeria, where he teaches African Poetry, Creative Writing and African Oral Literature. He has published three collections of poems and was the Africa region winner of the Commonwealth Poetry Prize in 1987.

Felicity Atuki Okoth: A freelance journalist in Nairobi, Kenya.

Isi Omoifo: A Nigerian journalist and writer.

Thembile ka Pepeteka: A writer in Port Elizabeth, South Africa.

Sobhna Keshavelal Poona: A student in South Africa.

Kofi Sam: A writer in Accra, Ghana.

Gloria Sandak-Lewin: A PhD student at the University of South Africa.

Erasmus Elikplim Forster Senaye: A writer in Accra, Ghana.

Michael Andrew Wakabi: A writer in Kampala, Uganda.

Timothy Wangusa: Professor of Literature at Makerere University, Uganda, who has published a collection of poems, *Salutations* (East African Literature Bureau, 1977) and a novel *Upon this Mountain* (Heinemann, 1989).

Sam Ukala: A Nigerian lecturer, playwright, dramatist and author of *The Slave Wife*.

Willie T. Zingani: A Malawian journalist, poet and novelist who has published works in Chichewa (Malawi's main vernacular language) and English. He works for World Vision International, Malawi.

THE AFRICAN AND CARIBBEAN WRITERS SERIES

The book you have been reading is part of Heinemann's long established series of African and Caribbean fiction. Details of some of the other titles available are given below, but for further information write to: Heinemann International, Halley Court, Jordan Hill, Oxford, OX2 8EJ.

KOJO LAING
GODHORSE

A powerful, witty and original collection of poems which must be the leading contender for the Commonwealth Poetry Prize in 1989. Kojo Laing's 'unique and individual voice' (Adam Lively) has produced a volume that is varied, inventive, evocative and often humorous.

SUMMER FIRES

New Poetry from Africa
Edited by Angus Calder, Jack Mapanje and Cosmo Pieterse
'Summer Fires is full of such exiting and provocative images, rooted in particular realities but coalescing to create a fantastic portrait of a continent . . .' *Stewart Brown*.

DENNIS BRUTUS
A Simple Lust

Letters to Martha appear in this book of his collected verse along with *Sirens Knuckles Boots* and *Poems from Algiers* and a wide range of his other poetry.

EDITED BY CHINUA ACHEBE
AND C. L. INNES
African Short Stories

Stories from West, East, North and Southern Africa which unite established figures such as Nadine Gordimer and Ngũgĩ wa Thiong'o with lesser-known, younger writers.

'A fine anthology, well-selected, well ordered, and altogether a pleasure to read.' *World Literature Today*

T. OBINKARAM ECHEWA
The Crippled Dancer

A novel of feud and intrigue set in Nigeria, by the winner of the English Speaking Union Literature Prize.

SEMBENE OUSMANE
God's Bits of Wood

The story of a strike on the Niger-Dakar railway, by the man who wrote and filmed *Xala*.

'Falling in the middle of Ousmane's literary canon, before he turned to film making, it is in some ways his most outstanding, and certainly his most ambitious work of fiction.' *West Africa*

RICHARD RIVE
Buckingham Palace District Six

'Buckingham Palace' is dingy row of five cottages in Cape Town's notorious District Six. The neighbourhood is enlivened by a bizarre and colourful cast of characters, including Mary, the brothel keeper, Katzen, the Jewish landlord and Zoot, the charismatic 'jive king' of the area.

ALEX LA GUMA
A Walk in the Night

Seven stories of decay, violence and poverty from the streets of Cape Town by one of South Africa's most impressive writers.

Time of the Butcherbird

In the intensifying summer heat, different members of a rural mining town community move inexorably towards conflict and ultimate tragedy. The time of the butcherbird is approaching. 'A most readable and moving book.' *West Africa*

BESSIE HEAD
Maru

Margaret Cadmore, an orphaned Masarwa girl, comes to Dilepe to teach, only to discover that even in this remote Botswana village her own people are treated as outcasts.

'I wanted the novel to be so beautiful and so magical that I, as the writer, would long to read and re-read it.' *Bessie Head*

A Question of Power

'She brilliantly develops ascending degrees of personal isolation, and is very moving when she describes abating pain. Her novels – and this is the third – have a way of soaring up from rock bottom to the stars, and are very shaking.' *The Sunday Times*